JUGGLING
STEP-BY-STEP

Bobby Besmehn

A STERLING/CHAPELLE BOOK

Sterling Publishing Co. Inc.   New York

This book is dedicated to anyone who has a dream, and especially to my family and the Harts. Thank you all for your support and encouragement through the years. Also, a special thanks goes out to Ms. Michelle Penman for being a good friend and for all the late nights you spent working on this book with me.

For Chapelle Ltd.

Owner: Jo Packham
Author: Bobby Besmehn
Editor: Cherie Hanson
Photographer: Ryne Hazen

Library of Congress Cataloging-in-Publication Data

Besmehn, Bobby.
　　Juggling step-by-step / by Bobby Besmehn.
　　　　p.　cm.
　　"A Sterling/Chapelle book."
　　Includes index.
　　ISBN 0-8069-0814-9
　　1. Juggling.　I. Title.
GV1558.B47　　1994
793.8'7—dc20　　　　　　　　　　　94–12873
　　　　　　　　　　　　　　　　　　　　　　CIP

10　9　8　7　6　5　4　3　2　1

A Sterling/Chapelle Book

Published by Sterling Publishing Company, Inc.
387 Park Avenue South, New York, N.Y. 10016
© 1994　by Chapelle Ltd.
Distributed in Canada by Sterling Publishing
$^{c}/o$ Canadian Manda Group, One Atlantic Avenue, Suite 105
Toronto, Ontario, Canada M6K 3E7
Distributed in Great Britain and Europe by Cassell PLC
Villiers House, 41/47 Strand, London WC2N 5JE, England
Distributed in Australia by Capricorn Link (Australia) Pty Ltd.
P.O. Box 6651, Baulkham Hills, Business Center, NSW 2153, Australia
Printed and bound in Hong Kong

Sterling ISBN 0-8069-0814-9

Introduction

Juggling is great fun! It's good exercise for your eyes and the rest of your body as well. It builds hand-eye coordination and can be very relaxing.

If you have dedication and ten free minutes a day for a week, you can join the millions who have learned to juggle.

All the information in this book is easy to follow, with color photos and path tracing arrows. The solid portion of the path represents the time the object you are juggling is in the air; the dotted lines represent the time the object is in your hand.

Before attempting each juggling technique, read through each sequence of steps. There is a small glossary at the end of the book if you come across terms you are not familiar with.

Welcome to the world of Juggling!

Contents

Chapter One — Scarves **5**
    Cascade 6
    Reverse Cascade 17
    Half Reverse 19
    Juggler's Tennis 20

Chapter Two — Balls **22**
    Cascade (One Ball) 23
    Cascade (Two Balls) 26
    Cascade (Three Balls) 29

Chapter Three — Assorted Ball Tricks 35
    Shower 36
    Columns 37
    The Fake 38
    The Yo-Yo 40
    Clawing 41
    Behind Your Back 42
    Flashy Start 48
    Neck Catch 50

Chapter Four — Juggling Other Items 51
    Juggling with Household Items 52
    Eating an Apple 53

Chapter Five — Tricks for Two **58**
    Two-Person Cascade 59
    Two-Person Pass 62

Chapter Six — Rings **68**
    Rings 69

Chapter Seven — Clubs **71**
    Clubs 72

Glossary **78**
Index **79**

Step 1   Cascade (One Scarf)

Begin with one scarf in your dominant hand. Hold it, with your palm down, between your thumb, first, and second fingers. The backs of your hands should be visible to you.

With a scooping motion from outside to inside, toss the scarf. It should go across your center line and peak about eight inches above your head on the opposite side from which you threw it.

Catch it in your subordinate hand with your palm down.

Step 2   Cascade (One Scarf)

If the scarf went behind you, you carried it too far through the pattern. Next time, release it sooner.

If the scarf went too far out in front of you, or did not come up high enough, you need to carry it through the scooping motion, releasing it at a higher point.

Ideally, release the scarf at chest height.

Step 3   Cascade (One Scarf)

Now that you have caught the scarf, throw it back to your
dominant hand and catch it. It should peak at the same
height.

Step 4   Cascade (One Scarf)

Now, throw the scarf back to your subordinate hand, then back to your dominant hand.

If you look at the picture above, you will notice the figure-eight pattern. This is very important to maintain.

Continue tossing the scarf back and forth from hand to hand until you have a steady rhythm. Practice starting with your subordinate hand also.

Step 5   Cascade (Two Scarves)

Now, start with one scarf in each hand, holding them between your thumb, first, and second fingers.

Call the scarf in your dominant hand "scarf #1," and the scarf in your subordinate hand "scarf #2."

Step 6   Cascade (Two Scarves)

Toss scarf #1 as practiced before, scooping outside to inside.

When scarf #1 reaches its peak, throw scarf #2 in the same manner. Catch both scarves and stop.

Step 7   Cascade (Two Scarves)

The scarves should have landed in opposite hands. Scarf #1 is now in your subordinate hand and scarf #2 is in your dominant hand.

Now throw scarf #1 from your subordinate hand back to your dominant hand. When it reaches its peak, throw scarf #2 back to your subordinate hand.

Practice this until you are consistent starting with each hand.

Step 8   Cascade (Three Scarves)

Hold two scarves in your dominant hand, one held between your first and second fingers, and the other between your thumb and first finger (this is the first scarf you throw). Hold another scarf in your subordinate hand.

Toss it as you have been practicing, scooping from the outside to the inside.

Step 9   Cascade (Three Scarves)

When scarf #1 reaches its peak, throw scarf #2, which is held between the thumb and first finger of your subordinate hand. It should peak at the same height as scarf #1.

Remember, when you throw with your left hand, the scarf should peak on your right side. When you throw with your right hand, it should peak on your left side.

Step 10   Cascade (Three Scarves)

As scarf #2 reaches its peak, throw scarf #3.

By this time you should have caught scarf #1 in the opposite hand from which you threw it.

Step 11   Cascade (Three Scarves)

Scarf #3 should be reaching its peak, and on its way to your subordinate hand which is holding scarf #1. Throw scarf #1.

Each time a scarf peaks, throw the next. Continue in this manner and before you know it, you are juggling!

Step 1   Reverse Cascade

You are ready for more!

Begin by tossing one scarf back and forth from hand to hand. But this time, instead of scooping the scarf from the outside to the inside, carry it from the inside out so that it makes the pattern shown above. We can call this throw "Over the Top."

Step 2   Reverse Cascade

Now, try it with two scarves. Practice starting with your subordinate and dominant hands alternating.

Then, try it with three scarves. Remember to use the outward scooping motion and to throw each time a scarf reaches its peak. The pattern should look like the one above.

Half Reverse

Each time a scarf hits your dominant hand, you toss it over the top with an inside to outside scooping motion.

Every scarf which reaches your subordinate hand, throw a regular cascade.

You can throw the scarves over the top extra high to allow yourself more time.

Juggler's Tennis

This is a variation that takes a little practice. As you are juggling in a cascade pattern, choose one of your scarves to throw in a reverse cascade pattern.

Make your next two throws as you would in a normal cascade pattern.

As the scarf you throw over the top comes down to your subordinate hand, throw it back over the top and make your next two throws continue in this way.

The same scarf goes over the top every time.

Tip to Remember

Never throw scarves palm up. You should always be able
to see the backs of your hands.

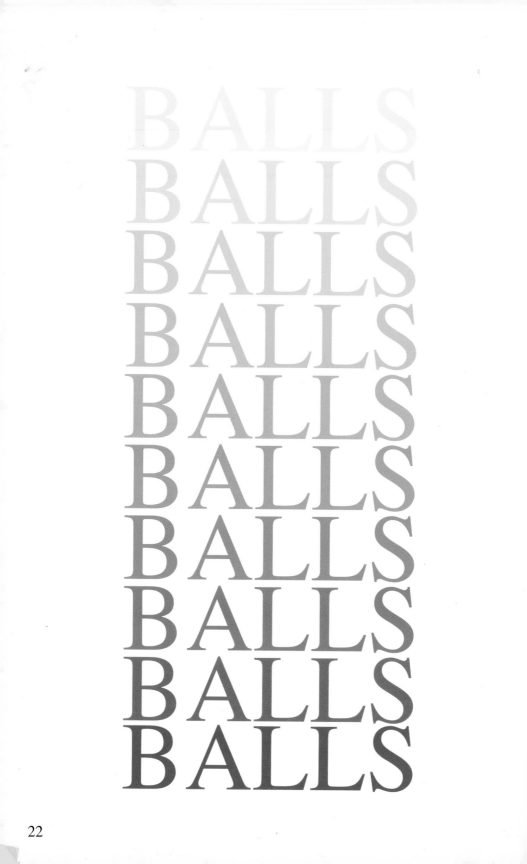

Step 1   Cascade (One Ball)

Hold the ball cradled in the palm of your dominant hand.

Make a scooping motion from outside to inside as you throw the ball. Release the ball just as it crosses your center line. Catch it in your other hand.

You want the ball to peak about 8 to 10 inches above your head.

stand up straight for balance

Step 2   Cascade (One Ball)

Now go through the same motions starting with your subordinate hand.

Allow the ball to roll from your palm to the middle of your fingers as you release it.

Catch it in your palm.

Your palm should always remain up.

Step 3   Cascade (One Ball)

Keep in mind that balls thrown from the right hand should peak left of your center line—balls thrown from the left hand should peak right of your center line.

Practice this until you can accurately throw the ball from hand to hand, maintaining a steady rhythm. Remember to make a scooping motion with each throw.

Step 1   Cascade (Two Balls)

Cradle one ball in each hand.

Your going to use the same scooping principle for juggling two balls as you did with one.

Toss a ball from your dominant hand. This time, when it reaches the top of its arc or peak, you throw the ball in the other hand. It should cross under the first ball and peak at the same height.

Step 2   Cascade (Two Balls)

When the step is complete, the balls should be in opposite hands.

The pictures above show examples of juggling using the scooping motion correctly and incorrectly.

Both balls should remain in the same plane, as in the figure on the left. Otherwise you will either end up chasing the balls or have a much harder time catching them.

Juggling takes place in two dimensions—height and width, not depth.

Step 3 Cascade (Two Balls)

Practice starting with your subordinate hand. If you were throwing right then left, now throw left then right. Practice this until you can do it consistently.

Then try alternating right, left, stop; then left, right stop; and so on.

You are trying to build a throw, throw-catch, catch rhythm.

Step 1   Cascade (Three Balls)

Start by holding two balls in your dominant hand and one ball in your subordinate hand.

The balls in your dominant hand should be held as such: one ball should be cradled deep within your palm and held in position with your third and fourth fingers. The second ball should be held in front with your thumb, first, and second fingers. This is the first ball thrown.

Step 2   Cascade (Three Balls)

Throw the first ball from your dominant hand. When it reaches its peak, you throw the single ball from your other hand.

As soon as this ball reaches it's peak, throw the remaining ball and stop.

Step 3   Cascade (Three Balls)

All balls should be on opposite sides from where they started.

If this worked the first try, you are doing great. If not, do not get discouraged. With a little more practice, you will find it quite easy. On the next page are a few pointers which might help.

Step 4   Cascade (Three Balls)

If you did not catch all the balls or could not even get them all out in sequence, try the following.

Throw the balls as described, only this time, do not worry about catching them. Just let them fall to the ground.

Your focus should be on when to throw, not how to catch. Each time a ball hits its peak, throw one from the other hand. After landing, the balls should be near your feet on opposite sides from which they began. Work on this for a while, then try to catch them again.

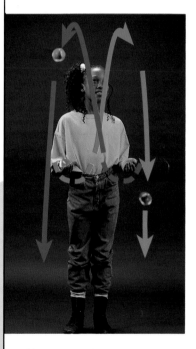 

If you got the balls out in sequence, but find yourself chasing them, try this.

Stand facing a wall, an arms length in front of you. This will help you confine your juggling in the two correct dimensions.

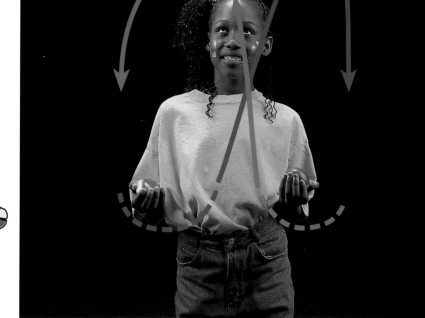

Step 5   Cascade (Three Balls)

Now try starting with your subordinate hand.

Try catching the balls. If you do not, then go through the same steps you went through when you started with your other hand.

After you can throw the balls starting with each hand, move on.

Step 6   Cascade (Three Balls)

Now begin as you did before, starting with your dominant hand. This time, when the third ball reaches its peak, the first ball should be in your subordinate hand. Toss this ball back to your dominant hand and continue throwing a ball every time a ball reaches its peak.

BALL TRICKS

BALL TRICKS

BALL TRICKS

BALL TRICKS

BALL TRICKS

BALL TRICKS

BALL TRICKS

BALL TRICKS

BALL TRICKS

BALL TRICKS

36

Shower (Two Balls in One Hand)

Begin with two balls in your dominant hand. With a scooping motion, throw one ball up, just a little higher than you normally do. Instead of crossing your center line, the ball should shoot right up the side of it.

When the ball reaches its peak, throw the second ball in the same manner.

Now, every time a ball reaches its peak, throw the next one. If you have problems making the balls circle, you might want to try the pattern on the next page.

3

Columns

The idea is the same as the two-ball shower, except, instead of chasing each other in a circular pattern, the balls are thrown straight up, side by side, and continue to be thrown in this pattern without crossing.

Step 1 The Fake

Now, juggle two balls in either the shower or column pattern while holding a third ball in your subordinate hand.

You should hold the third ball with your fingertips. Your palm should be facing forward as if you are showing it to your audience.

Now, as you juggle, try looking at the third ball. Practice this until it is easy. Doing this may sound silly, but you will find it very helpful for learning this trick.

Step 2   The Fake

Now, rather than simply holding the third ball, you are going to pick one of the two balls your are juggling and track it with the third ball held in your hand.

When you throw the ball you are tracking up, your hand should move up beside it. As the ball comes down, your hand comes down with it

If you have this timed right, it should take a couple of seconds for your audience to figure out that you are not actually juggling.

The Yo-Yo

To do the Yo-Yo, juggle two balls using the column pattern on page 37. You are going to be tracking a ball as in the fake on pages 38–39 but instead of faking at the side of the ball, you will be above it.

Try imagining a piece of string joining the two balls together and it is your job to keep the string tight. This will create the illusion that the two balls are hooked together.

4

Clawing

Here is a trick that is quite easy to learn. When performed quickly, it is very flashy.

Instead of juggling with your palms up, juggle with your palms forward.

If you study the picture, you will notice that an outside to inside scooping pattern is still used.

In the beginning, practice with one ball, then two balls, then finally three balls.

Step 1   Behind Your Back

Begin with one ball in your dominant hand.

In one consistent movement, bring the ball around you and
throw it over your opposite shoulder, catching it with your
subordinate hand.

Step 2   Behind Your Back

If you have problems, here are a few ideas you might keep in mind as you practice.

Carry the ball as far around and up your back as possible before releasing it.

Most importantly, before and as you throw, think about catching the ball more than throwing it.

As you gain control, start throwing the ball different heights. Practice throwing with your subordinate hand also.

Step 3   Behind Your Back

Now, try using two balls.

Throw one ball behind your back. When it reaches its peak, throw the other ball in front of you in a cascade pattern.

Practice this until you can do it consistently.

Remember to pause after every second throw. The pause is the place in which the third ball would normally be thrown.

Step 4   Behind Your Back

Now, throw the ball from your subordinate hand first in a cascade. You can throw this ball extra high to allow yourself more time to make the pass behind your back.

If you are doing this correctly, you will not see the ball you are catching with your dominant hand because you are focused on the ball coming around your head.

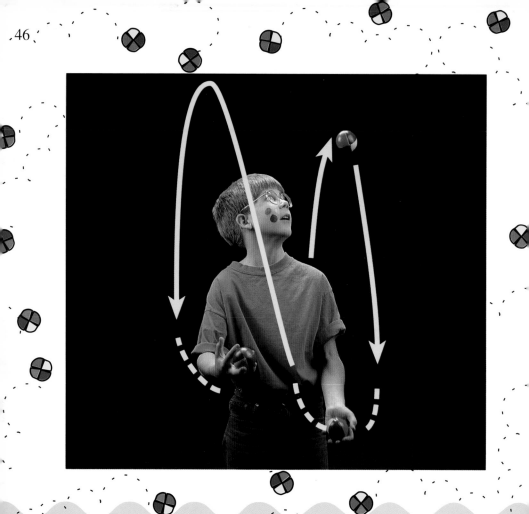

Step 5   Behind Your Back

Now, begin to juggle three balls in a cascade.

Throw a ball from your subordinate hand higher than you normally would. The ball which immediately follows this, thrown from your dominant hand, is the ball which you pass behind your back.

Step 6   Behind Your Back

There is no set height at which you must throw the ball behind your back. You can throw it high or low. As long as you throw it straight up, you will be able to catch it and continue juggling.

As your behind the back throw becomes faster, you will be able to bring the "high ball" down to the height of your regular pattern.

Although this trick may seem difficult at first, with practice, it will become so natural that you do not even think about it. In a short while, you can be doing tricks like "back crosses"—throwing every ball from each hand behind your back. It only takes practice.

Step 1   Flashy Start (Three Balls)

Begin by placing all three balls in your dominant hand. Two balls should be side by side and near your body. Hold them in place with your thumb and pinky finger. The third ball should be in front of them and held with your first three fingers only.

Scoop the balls straight up near the center of your body. Keep your first three fingers stiff as you throw the balls; they will act as a ramp for the first ball.

Hint: Exaggerate the scooping motion by flipping your wrist.

Step 2   Flashy Start (Three Balls)

The ball in front will travel higher than the two behind it. As the balls reach their peaks, quickly claw the lower two and use the remaining high ball as your first throw to begin juggling.

You have to be fast, and it takes practice. Try using the same move to start the balls behind your back, under your leg, or over your shoulder.

Neck Catch

Throw one ball high. As it falls, bring your upper body down with it. At this point, you should roll your head back and lift your arms, creating a well, with the back of your neck as the bottom. This well is where you catch the ball. Continue moving your upper body downward, stopping gradually as the ball reaches your neck. Do not stop suddenly, or the ball will bounce out.

OTHER ITEMS

OTHER ITEMS

OTHER ITEMS

OTHER ITEMS

OTHER ITEMS

OTHER ITEMS

OTHER ITEMS

OTHER ITEMS

OTHER ITEMS

OTHER ITEMS

Juggling with Household Items

Rolled-up socks are great for juggling around the house. Tennis balls will work as well. Apples, oranges and other assorted fruits are fun, but make sure you have permission from your parents when juggling with food.

Step 1   Eating an Apple

To avoid the senseless slaughter of thousands of apples, you should practice these moves with balls before trying it with the apple.

If you can hold a three-ball cascade easily, this trick should come with little effort. It is a classic comedy juggling routine, and, when presented well, it is a trick capable of entertaining any audience.

Step 2   Eating an Apple

Begin juggling three balls in a cascade pattern. Choose one of the balls to represent your apple. When the "apple" ball reaches your dominant hand, throw the ball in your subordinate hand extra high. This gives you time to then kiss the ball that represents the apple, and throw it back into the pattern.

Kissing the ball creates the timing and movement you need to take a bite of the actual apple when you use it.

Step 3   Eating an Apple

Remember to catch the highest ball with your dominant hand and toss the "apple" ball to your subordinate hand.

At first, kiss the ball every second or third time it reaches your dominant hand.

Step 4   Eating an Apple

Gradually work towards throwing the highest ball lower and lower, until it is the same height as the rest of the balls in your pattern or ss the ball each time it reaches your dominant h?

If you practice, you will be able to kiss the "apple" ball each time you catch it, using both your subordinate and dominant hands.

Step 5   Eating an Apple (Preparation)

Tips

Remove the stem from the apple and check for worm holes before performing the trick. You do not want any surprises.

Your hands will become sticky as you continue to handle the apple you have bitten into. So, whatever else you are juggling with will become sticky as well. Choose balls to juggle that are easy to clean.

Step 6   Eating an Apple (Performance)

When performing, it works well to start as you did when you first learned. Take a bite every second or third time the apple reaches your dominant hand. The first time you take a bite, make it look extremely difficult and act as if you have just done the world's greatest trick. Then, gradually work towards taking a bite each time the apple reaches your dominant hand. Your audience will be amazed and they will probably be falling out of their seats from laughter.

TRICKS FOR TWO

TRICKS FOR TWO

TRICKS FOR TWO

TRICKS FOR TWO

TRICKS FOR TWO

TRICKS FOR TWO

TRICKS FOR TWO

TRICKS FOR TWO

TRICKS FOR TWO

TRICKS FOR TWO

Step 1   Two-Person Cascade

Juggling with a friend can be fun! Stand side by side; you can put your arms around each other if you like. (In most cases, this helps in the beginning.)

Practice tossing one ball back and forth. The person on the left uses his or her left hand and the person on the right uses his or her right hand.

Toss the ball the same height as you would for juggling three balls by yourself. Your throws must be accurate for your partner to catch them. And, you must both throw the ball the same height to maintain a steady rhythm.

Step 2   Two-Person Cascade

Now, try it with two balls. The person on the right throws first. When the ball reaches its peak, the person on the left throws.

Next, try reversing it. The person on the left throws first. When the ball reaches its peak, the person on the right throws.

Now, try using three balls. You are just doing a cascade pattern, so each time a ball reaches its peak, throw the next one.

Step 3   Two-Person Cascade

If both of you can already juggle, you will find this quite easy and soon be able to do tricks like tennis or reverse cascade.

Bring the pattern down low, then up high, or just see how long you can go!

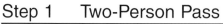

Step 1   Two-Person Pass

To begin, stand facing your partner. Stand about three feet from each other. Each of you holds a ball in your right hand.

Pass the balls straight across, catching them in your left hand. The balls should peak just above eye level.

Now each of you throws the ball in your left hand to your right hand. Then repeat the steps above.

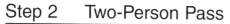

Step 2   Two-Person Pass

Practicing the move on this page may help your passing more than anything. You can try it with someone who knows how to juggle or even a friend who does not.

Hold one ball in each hand. Your partner throws you a third ball, as practiced on the previous page. Begin juggling.

Throw the ball from your left hand when the ball your partner throws reaches its peak.

Step 3   Two-Person Pass

When each of you can easily start when having a ball thrown in, try using three balls each.

Two balls should be held in your right hands and the other one in your left hands. Your arms should be in front of you and bent at the elbows.

Drop your arms together and immediately pass the first ball from your right hand. Begin to juggle.

Make two throws to yourself from your right hand and pass again.

Step 4   Two-Person Pass

To make this pattern easier to follow, use four balls of one color and two of another color. Both of you start by passing the odd-colored ball; then every time an odd-colored ball reaches your right hand, pass it. When you can pass every third ball consistently, try passing every other ball.

Start the same as you did before; then, instead of making two self throws from your right hand, only make one.

The pattern goes pass, self throw, pass, self throw, pass, and so on. The red arrows show the height at which your self throws should peak.

Step 5   Two-Person Pass

This next pattern takes a little more practice, but most can learn it in a week or less.

Warm up by practicing the patterns on the previous pages.

Now, start with a pass; then, every time a ball reaches your right hand, pass it.

Step 1   Rings

Juggling rings is similar to juggling balls. You still use a cascade pattern.

Your palms should be facing each other.

As with most other juggling movements, start with one object, then work your way to using more.

Step 2   Rings

Although the scooping motion from outside to inside is the same, notice when the ring is released, it is turned slightly to the inside. This helps it to cross your other hand.

Rings (Common Problems)

When starting with more than one ring in your hand,
you should place a finger between each ring. You will find
you have more control in making your first throws.

If you are chasing rings, you are releasing the rings too
soon. Try to put a backspin on the rings as you throw them.

CLUBS
CLUBS
CLUBS
CLUBS
CLUBS
CLUBS
CLUBS
CLUBS
CLUBS
CLUBS

Step 1   Clubs

Begin with one club in your dominant hand.

Hold it near the middle of the handle. Notice the hand and arm positions.

The clubs should be held palms-up and turned to a 45-degree angle from your shoulders.

Step 2   Clubs

Next, make a 90-degree scooping motion and release the club.

The club should make one complete rotation, peaking about a foot above your head and landing at a 45-degree angle in your other hand.

Step 3   Clubs

Now try starting with your other hand. Practice this until
you can hold a steady rhythm of right, left, right, left, and
so on.

Step 4   Clubs

Now, hold one club in each hand.

Throw the club in your dominant hand. When the club peaks, throw the club in your subordinate hand.

It is just like juggling balls or rings, except each club has to make one complete rotation before you catch it.

Repeat this pattern until you become proficient starting with both hands.

Step 5   Clubs

To begin juggling three clubs, you may want to practice holding two clubs in one hand.

The three-club start can be a little tricky, so study the club and finger positions holding two clubs in one hand. You will notice the knob of the first club is on top and your index finger rests on the bottom of this club.

You might want to practice by starting with two clubs in one hand and nothing in the other until you get the hang of the first throw.

Step 6   Clubs

Now begin to juggle—right, left, right, left. Throw a club each time one club peaks.

Here is a tip for club juggling in the future.

Whenever you make a body throw, such as under the leg or behind your back, you want to let your hand slip down the knob of the club as you release it.

As a reminder, be aware of what you are doing and do not make the same mistake twice.

Glossary

Ball: A round object used in juggling. Usually made of rubber.

Bean Bag: Juggling object often round or square shaped and about 2" diameter. It is filled with rice or bird seed.

Cascade: Basic juggling pattern in which objects thrown from your right hand peak left of your center line, and objects thrown from your left hand peak right of your center line.

Center Line: An imaginary line which runs up the center of your body. It connects with the ground and stretches high over your head.

Club: A fairly advanced jugglers prop. It is shaped much like a bowling pin and is weighted specially for juggling.

Dominant Hand: The hand you eat with, write with, and generally use the most.

Peak: The highest point an object reaches when it is thrown.

Ring: A flat, disc-shaped juggling prop. Usually about an eighth of an inch in thickness and 13" diameter.

Scarf: Lightweight cloth used for juggling. It is considered to be the easiest object to juggle.

Self Throw: A term used mostly when passing. It represents the throws to yourself from the passing hand.

Subordinate Hand: The hand which you use the least.

Index

ball 78
bean bag 78
behind your back 42
cascade 78
    balls (one)........................... 23
    balls (three) 29
    balls (two) 26
    scarves (one)........................ 6
    scarves (three) 13
    scarves (two) 10
    two-person.......................... 59
center line 78
clawing 41
club(s) 72, 78
columns 37
dominant hand 78
eating an apple 53
fake, the 38
flashy start 48
half reverse (scarves) 19
household items...................... 52
juggler's tennis (scarves) 20
neck catch 50
peak 78
reverse cascade (scarves) 17
ring(s)............................... 68, 78
self throw 78
scarf 78
shower 36
subordinate hand 78
two-person cascade 59
two-person pass 62
yo-yo, the 40

About the Author

The author, Bobby Besmehn, has been juggling since his 13th birthday when his parents bought him his first set of juggling clubs.

Presently, Mr. Besmehn travels North America starring in the Shrine Circus. He also entertains for Disabled American Veterans benefits, Police Association benefits, state fairs, hotel conventions, and casinos.

He loves to juggle and practices hours daily.

JUL 2 9 '96